ROBERT JOHNSON

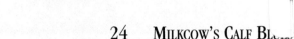

Easy Guitar Collection

Contents

Robert Johnson photo booth self-portrait, ca. early 1930s
© 1986 Delta Haze Corporation

ISBN 978-0-634-06432-6

HAL•LEONARD®
CORPORATION

7777 W. BLUEMOUND RD. P.O. BOX 13819 MILWAUKEE, WI 53213

Visit Hal Leonard Online at
www.halleonard.com

Come on in My Kitchen

Words and Music by Robert Johnson

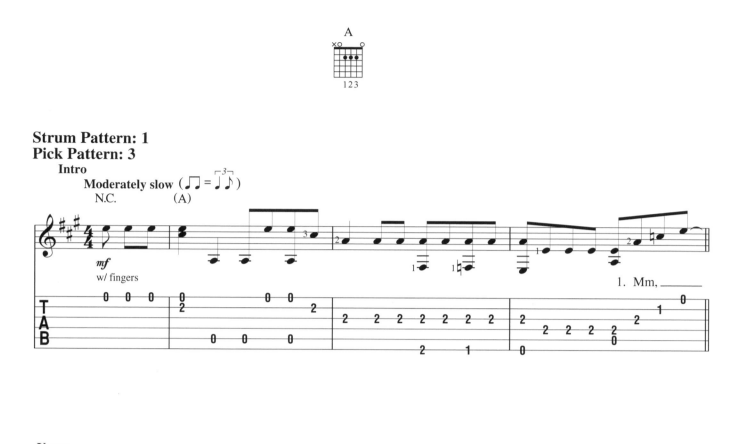

Strum Pattern: 1
Pick Pattern: 3

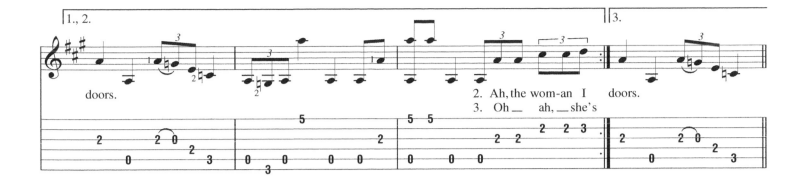

Bridge
A

Spoken: *Oh, can't you hear the wind howl?*   *Oh, can't you hear the wind howl?*   You bet-ter come on   in my

kitch - en.   Ba - by, it's gon' to be rain - in' out - doors.

Verse
A

4. When a wom-an gets in   trou - ble,   ev-'ry-bod-y throws her

down.   Look-in' for her good   friend,   none can be found.   You bet - ter   come on   in my

kitch-en.   Ba-by, it's gon' to be rain - in' out - doors.

Verse
A

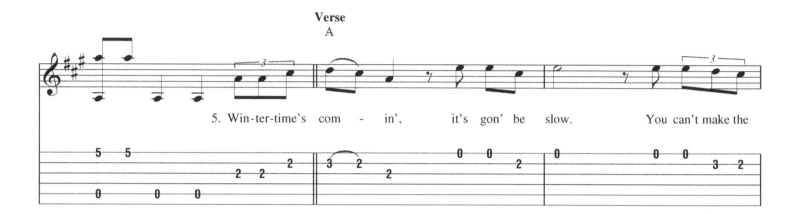

5. Win-ter-time's com - in',   it's gon' be   slow.   You can't make the

win- ter, babe,   that's dry long so.   You bet - ter come on   in my kitch-en   'cause _ it's

gon' to be rain - in' out - doors.

Kind Hearted Woman Blues

Words and Music by Robert Johnson

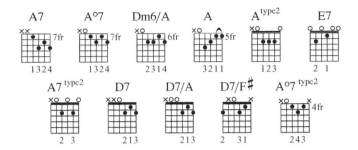

Strum Pattern: 1
Pick Pattern: 3

Intro
Moderately slow

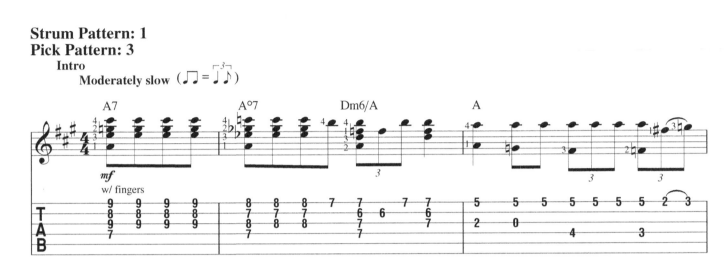

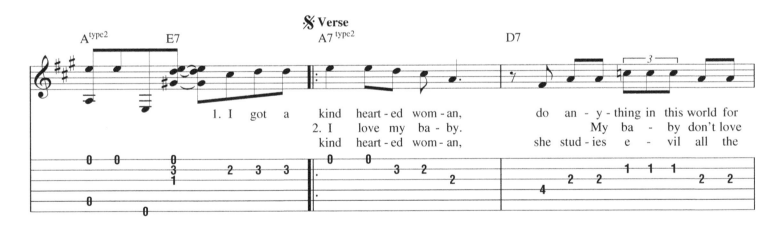

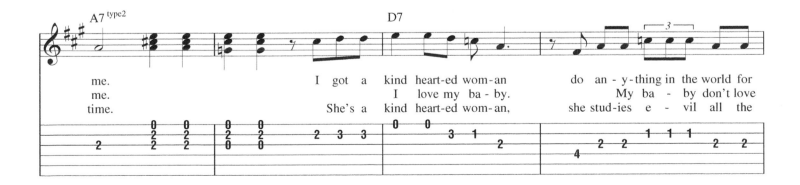

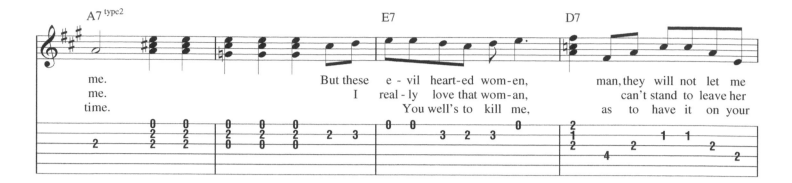

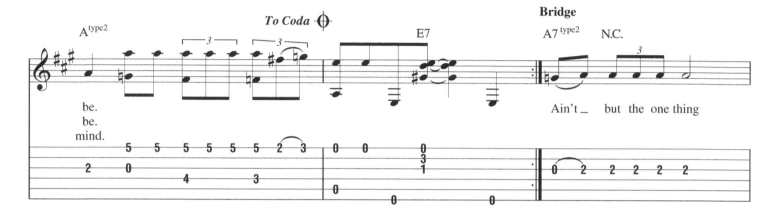

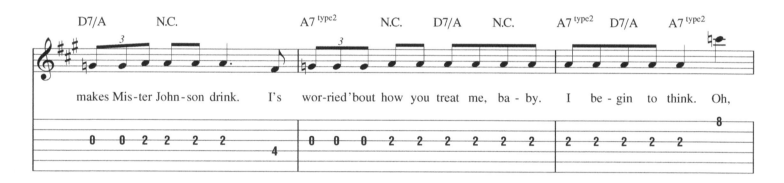

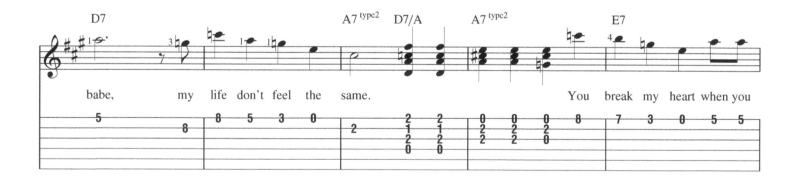

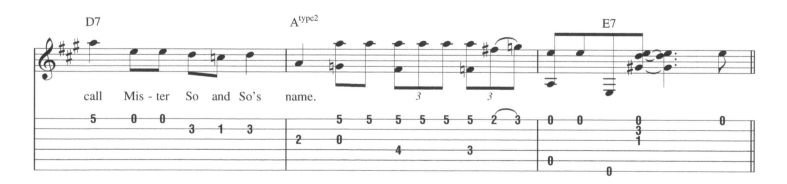

Guitar Solo

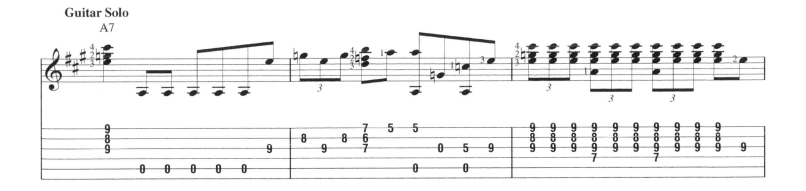

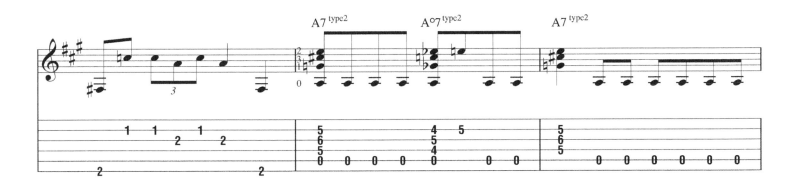

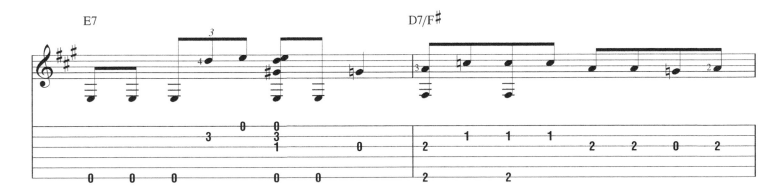

D.S. al Coda

⊕ Coda

3. She's a

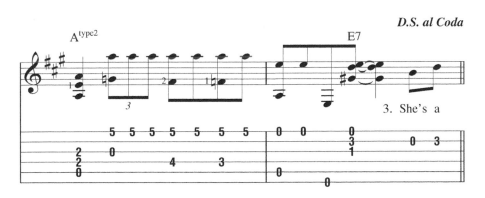

Cross Road Blues
(Crossroads)

Words and Music by Robert Johnson

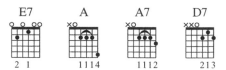

Strum Pattern: 1
Pick Pattern: 3

Intro
Moderately

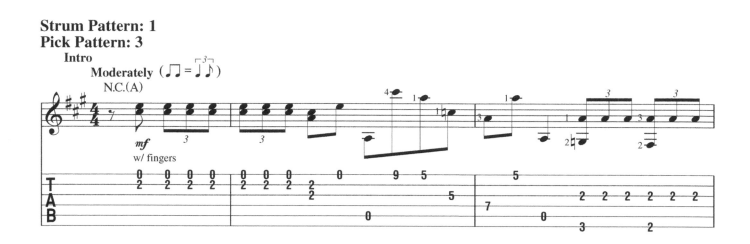

Verse

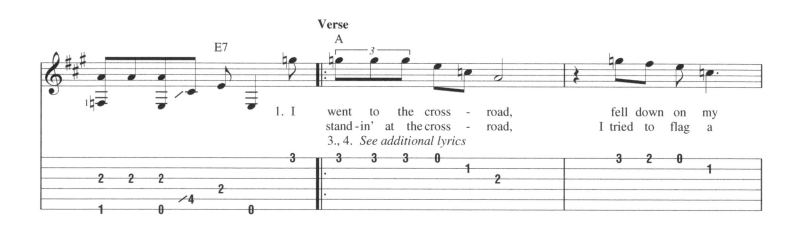

1. I went to the cross - road, fell down on my
stand - in' at the cross - road, I tried to flag a
3., 4. *See additional lyrics*

knees.
ride.
I went to the cross - road,
Stand - in' at the cross - road,

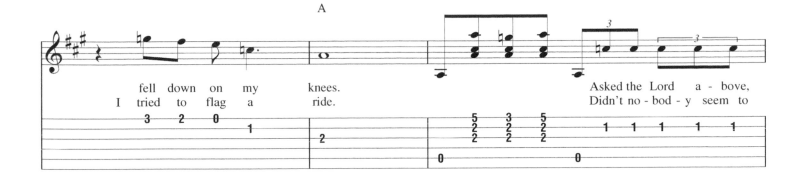

fell down on my knees.
I tried to flag a ride.

Asked the Lord a-bove,
Didn't no-bod-y seem to

E7   A   1., 2., 3.
                                           A7

"Have mer-cy.
know me,_____

Save poor Bob, if you please."
ev-'ry-bod-y pass me by.

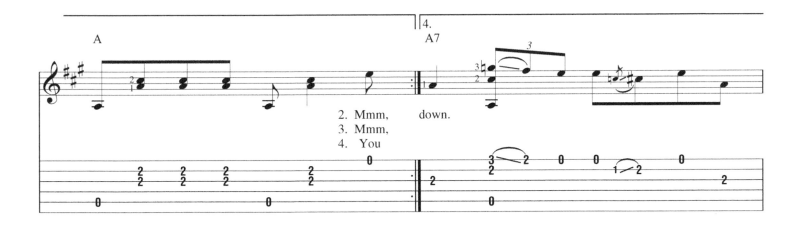

A   4.
                          A7

2. Mmm,   down.
3. Mmm,
4. You

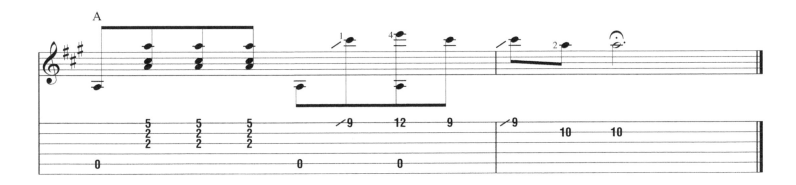

A

Additional Lyrics

3. Mmm, the sun goin' down, boy.
   Dark gon' catch me here.
   Oo eee, boy,
   Dark gon' catch me here.
   I haven't got no lovin' sweet woman,
   That love and feel my care.

4. You can run, you can run.
   Tell my friend-boy Willie Brown.
   You can run.
   Tell my friend-boy Willie Brown.
   Lord, that I'm standin' at the crossroad, babe,
   I believe I'm sinkin' down.

From Four Until Late

Words and Music by Robert Johnson

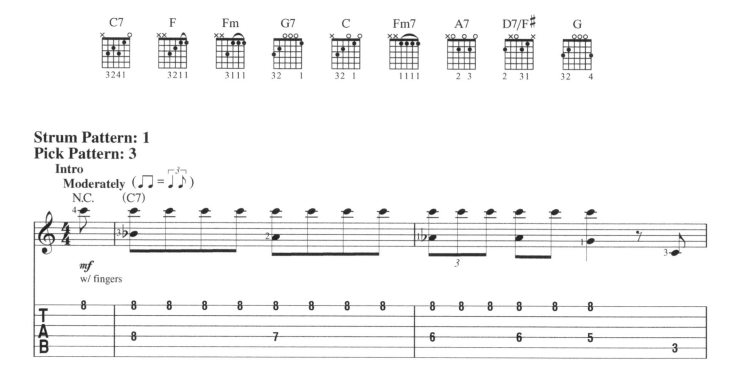

Strum Pattern: 1
Pick Pattern: 3

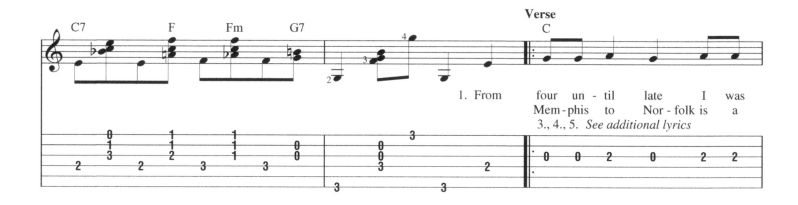

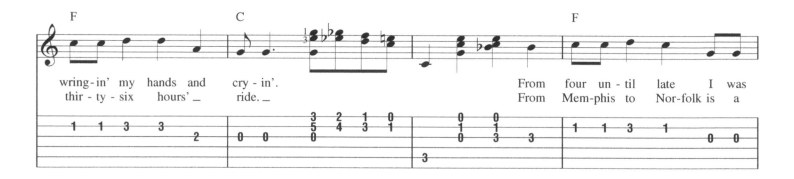

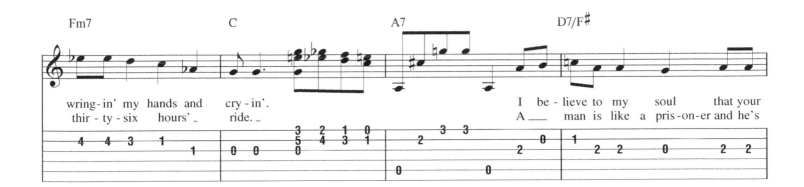

wring-in' my hands and cry - in'.
thir - ty - six hours'_ ride. _
I be - lieve to my soul that your
A_ man is like a pris-on-er and he's

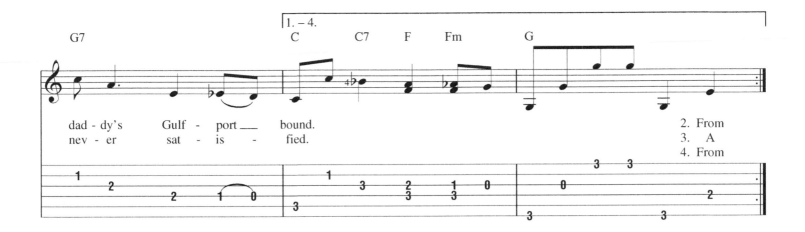

dad - dy's Gulf - port_ bound.
nev - er sat - is - fied.

2. From
3. A
4. From

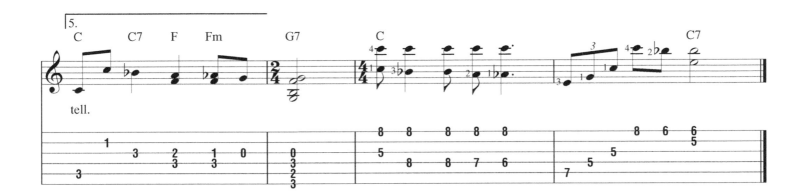

tell.

Additional Lyrics

3. A woman is like a dresser,
   Some man always ramblin' through its drawers.
   A woman is like a dresser,
   Some man's always ramblin' through its drawers.
   It cause so many men
   Wear an apron overhall.

4. From four until late,
   She get with a no-good bunch and clown.
   From four until late,
   She get with a no-good bunch and clown.
   Now she won't do nothin'
   But tear a good man' reputation down.

5. When I leave this town,
   I'm 'on' bid you fare ... farewell.
   And when I leave this town,
   I'm gon' bid you fare ... farewell.
   And when I return again,
   You'll have a great long story to tell.

Hell Hound on My Trail

Words and Music by Robert Johnson

hail.

And the day, it keeps on wor-'y'n' me. ___
All I would need, my lit-tle sweet rid-er just ___

It's a hell hound ___ on my trail. Hell hound on my trail. ___ Hell hound on my
to pass the time ___ a - way. Huh ___ huh, ___ to pass the time a -

trail.

way.

2. If to -
3. You sprin-kled
4. I can

Hey, ___

___ my com-pan - y.

Additional Lyrics

3. You sprinkled hot foot powder, mmm,
   Around my door, all around my door.
   You sprinkled hot foot powder all around your daddy's door.
   Hmm, hmm, hmm.
   It keeps me with a ramblin' mind, rider,
   Every old place I go, every old place I go.

4. I can tell the wind is risin',
   The leaves tremblin' on the tree, tremblin' on the tree.
   I can tell the wind is risin',
   The leaves tremblin' on the tree. Hmm, hmm, hmm.
   All I need's my little sweet woman,
   And to keep my company. Hey, my company.

I Believe I'll Dust My Broom

Words and Music by Robert Johnson

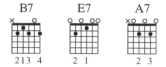

Strum Pattern: 1
Pick Pattern: 3

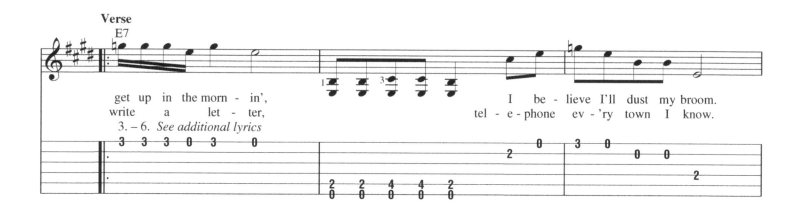

lieve I'll dust my broom.
ev - 'ry town I know.

Girl-friend, the black man you been lov - in',
If I can't fine her in West Hel - 'na',

girl - friend, can get my room.
she must be in East Mon-roe, I know.

2. I'm gon'
3. I don't
4. I be -

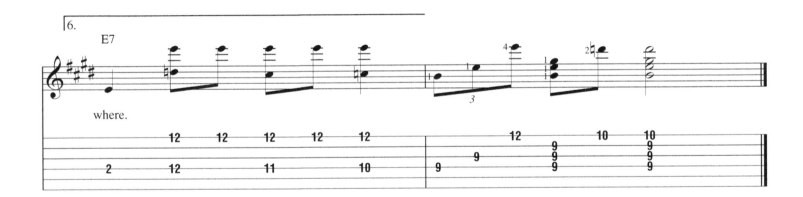

where.

Additional Lyrics

3. I don't want no woman,
   Wants every downtown man she meet.
   I don't want no woman,
   Wants every downtown man she meet.
   She's a no-good doney,
   They shouldn't 'low her on the street.

4. I believe,
   I believe I'll go back home.
   I believe,
   I believe I'll go back home.
   You can mistreat me here, babe,
   But you can`t when I go home.

5. And I'm gettin' up in the mornin'.
   I believe I'll dust my broom.
   I'm gettin' up in the mornin'.
   I believe I'll dust my broom.
   Girlfriend, the black man you been lovin',
   Girlfriend, can get my room.

6. I'm gon' call up Chiney,
   See is my good girl over there.
   I'm gon' call up China,
   See is my good girl over there.
   'F I can't find her on Philippine's Island,
   She must be in Ethiopia somewere.

I'm a Steady Rollin' Man
(Steady Rollin' Man)

Words and Music by Robert Johnson

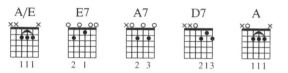

Strum Pattern: 1
Pick Pattern: 3

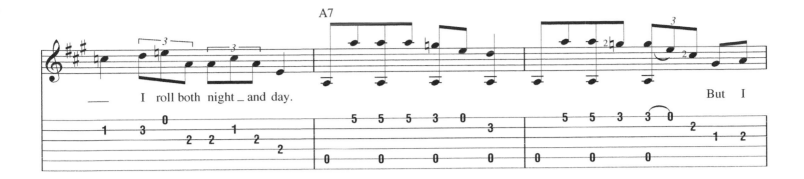

I roll both night _ and day.
But I

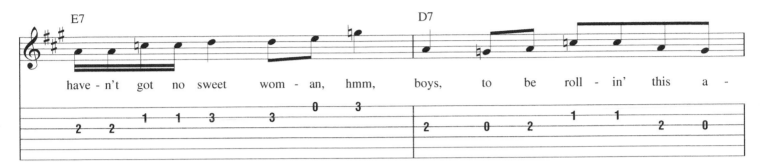

have - n't got no sweet wom - an, hmm, boys, to be roll - in' this a -

way.
2. I'm the way.
3. I'm a
4. You can't

Additional Lyrics

2. I'm the man that rolls
   When icicles is hangin' on the tree.
   I'm the man that rolls
   When icicles is hangin' on the tree.
   And now you hear me howlin', baby,
   Hmm, down on my bended knee.

3. I'm a hard workin' man,
   Have been for many years, I know.
   I'm a hard workin' man,
   Have been for many years, I know.
   And some cream puff's usin' my money, ooh,
   Well, babe, that'll never be no more.

4. You can't give your sweet woman
   Everything she wants in one time.
   Ooh, hoo, ooo, you can't give your sweet woman
   Everything she wants in one time.
   Well boys, she get ramblin' in her brain,
   Hmm, some monkey man on her mind.

Last Fair Deal Gone Down

Words and Music by Robert Johnson

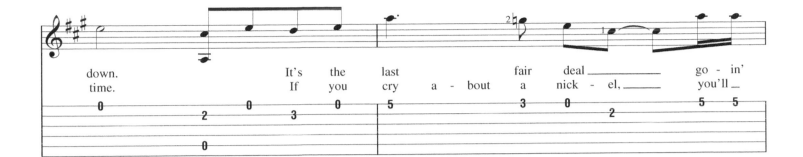

down.   It's the last   fair deal _____ go - in'
time.   If you cry a - bout a nick - el, _____ you'll __

down, _____ good __ Lord, on that Gulf - port Is - land
die _____ 'bout a dime. She would - n't cry, but the mon - ey won't

1. – 7.		8.

Road.   2. Eh, Road.
mind.   3. I

Additional Lyrics

3. I like y' way you do.
   I love the way you do.
   I love the way you do, good Lord,
   On this Gulfport Island Road.

4. My captain's so mean on me.
   My captain's so mean on me.
   My captain's so mean on m', mmm, good Lord,
   On this Gulfport Island Road.

5. They count, they pick and sing.
   Count, they pick and sing.
   Let's count and pick and sing, good Lord,
   On that Gulfport Island Road.

6. Ah, this last fair deal goin' down.
   It's the last fair deal goin' down.
   This' the last fair deal goin' down, good Lord,
   On this Gulfport Island Road.

7. I'm workin' my way back home.
   I'm workin' my way back home.
   I'm workin' my way back home, good Lord,
   On this Gulfport Island Road.

8. And that thing don't keep a ringin' so soon.
   That thing don't keep a ringin' so soon.
   And that thing don't keep a ringin' so soon, good Lord,
   On that Gulfport Island Road.

Love in Vain Blues

Words and Music by Robert Johnson

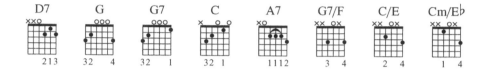

Strum Pattern: 1
Pick Pattern: 2

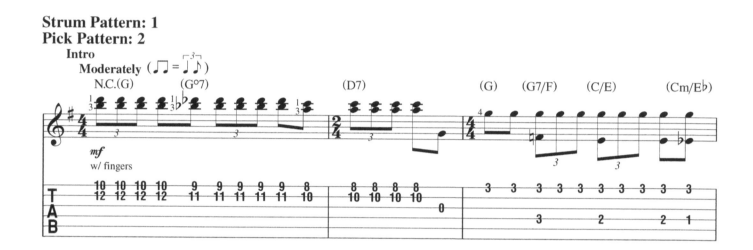

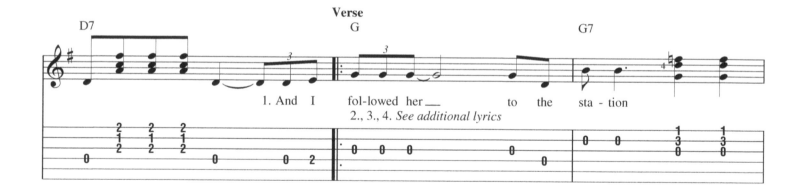

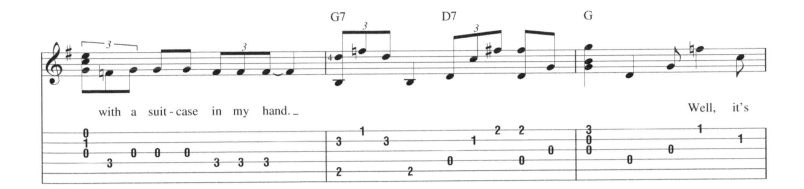

with a suit-case in my hand. ___ Well, it's

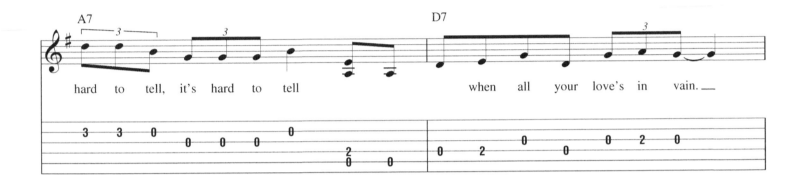

hard to tell, it's hard to tell when all your love's in vain. ___

All my love's in vain. 2. When the vain. ___
3. When the
4. Ou, ___

Additional Lyrics

2. When the train rolled up to the station,
   I looked her in the eye.
   When the train rolled up to the station,
   I looked her in the eye.
   Well, I was lonesome, I felt so lonesome
   And I could not help but cry. All my love's in vain.

3. When the train, it left the station
   With two lights on behind.
   When the train, it left the station
   With two lights on behind.
   Well, the blue light was my blues
   And the red light was my mind. All my love's in vain.

4. Ou, hou,
   Hoo, Willie Mae.
   Oh, oh, hey,
   Hoo, Willie Mae.
   Ou, ou, ou, ou,
   Hee, vee, oh woe. All my love's in vain.

Malted Milk

Words and Music by Robert Johnson

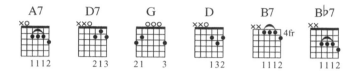

Strum Pattern: 1
Pick Pattern: 2

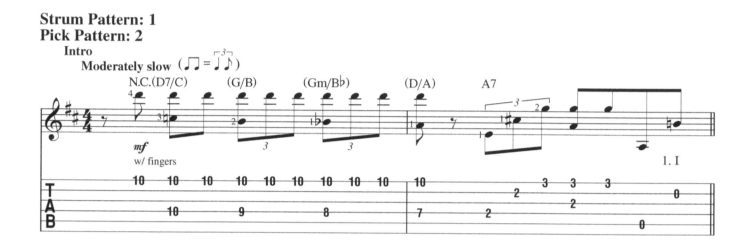

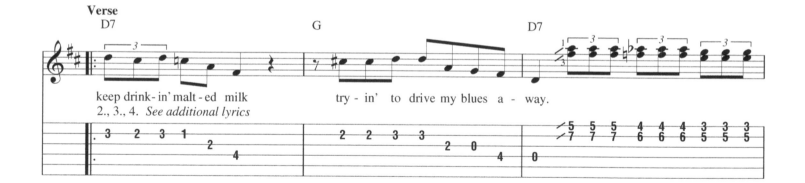

way. ___ Ba-by, you just as wel-come to my lov-in' as the

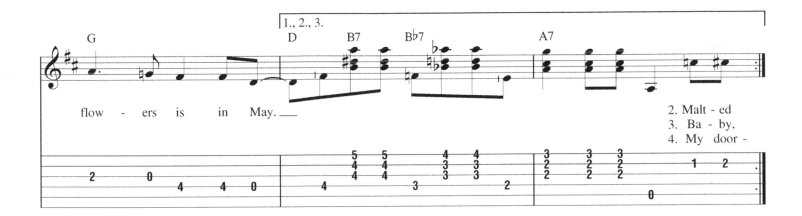

flow - ers is in May. ___

2. Malt - ed
3. Ba - by,
4. My door -

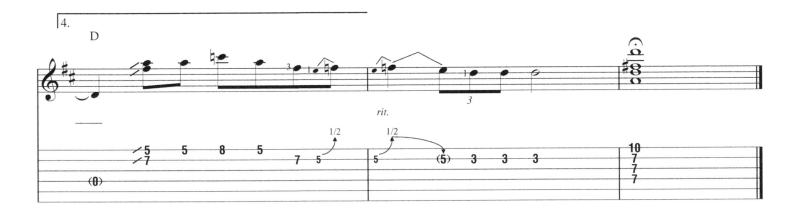

Additional Lyrics

2. Malted milk, malted milk
   Keep rushin' to my head.
   Malted milk, malted milk
   Keep rushin' to my head.
   And I have a funny, funny feelin'
   And I'm talkin' all out my head.

3. Baby, fix me one more drink
   And hug your daddy one more time.
   Baby, fix me one more drink
   And hug your daddy one more time.
   Keep on stirrin' in my malted milk, mama,
   Until I change my mind.

4. My doorknob keeps on turnin'.
   It must be spooks around my bed.
   My doorknob keeps on turnin'.
   Must be spooks around my bed.
   I have a warm, old feelin'
   And the hair risin' on my head.

Milkcow's Calf Blues

Words and Music by Robert Johnson

A7   D7   E7   A

Strum Pattern: 1
Pick Pattern: 3

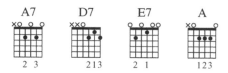

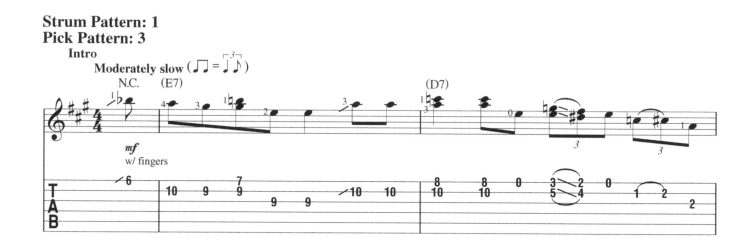

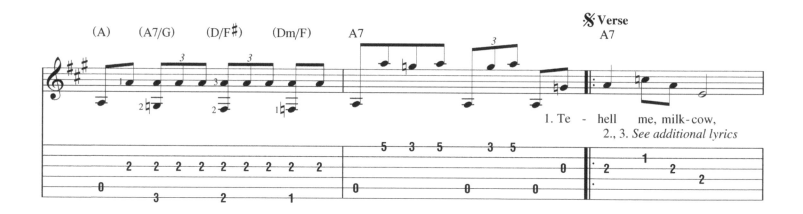

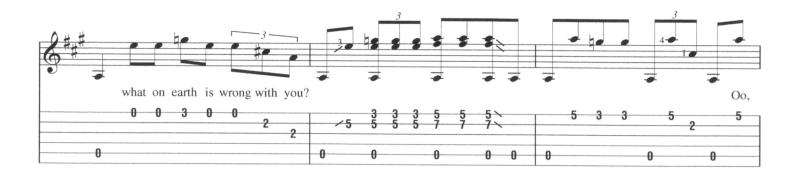

what on earth is wrong with you?

Oo,

ee, milk - cow, ___ what on earth is wrong with you?

To Coda

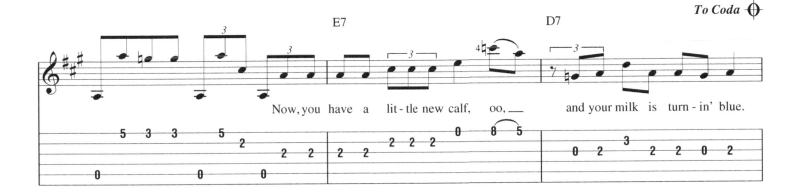

Now, you have a lit-tle new calf, oo, ___ and your milk is turn-in' blue.

2. Now, your

Bridge

Now I feel like milk-in' and my cow won't come. I feel like chu'n-in' and my

milk won't turn. __ I'm cry-in' plea - ease, plea - ease, don't do me wrong.

If you see my milk cow, ba - by now, __ how, __ please drive her home. __

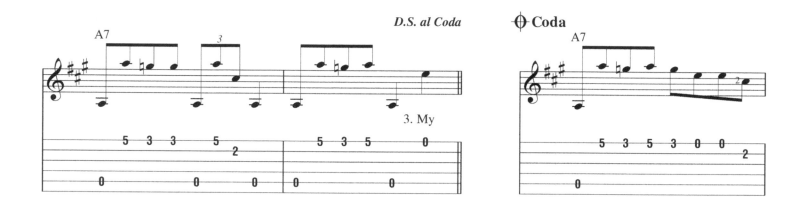

D.S. al Coda

Coda

3. My

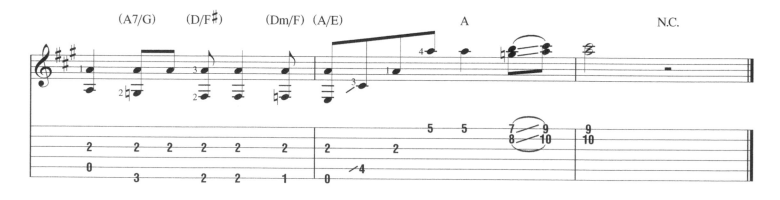

Additional Lyrics

2. Now, your calf is hungry.
   I believe he needs a suck.
   Now, your calf is hungry.
   Hoo, I believe he needs a suck.
   But your milk is turnin' blue.
   Hoo, I believe he's outta luck.

3. My milk cow been ramblin,'
   Hoo, hee, for miles around.
   My milk cow's been ramblin',
   Hoo, for miles around.
   Well, now she been suckin' some other man's bull cow,
   Hoo, in this strange man's town.

Phonograph Blues

Words and Music by Robert Johnson

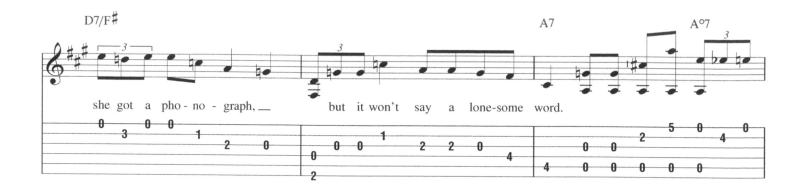

she got a pho - no - graph, __ but it won't say a lone-some word.

4th time, To Coda ⊕

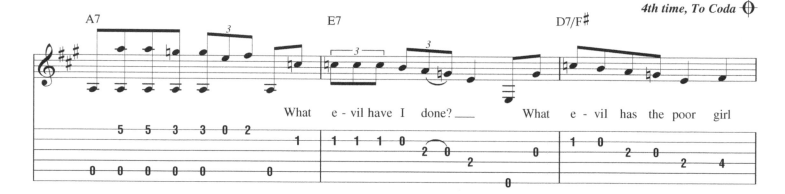

What e - vil have I done? __ What e - vil has the poor girl

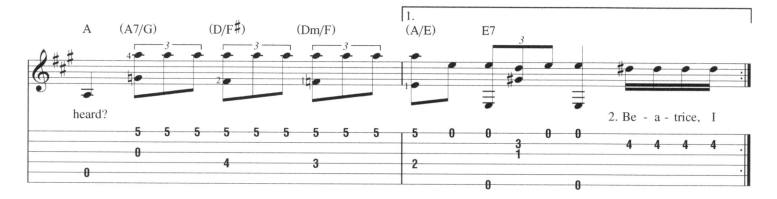

heard? 2. Be - a - trice, I

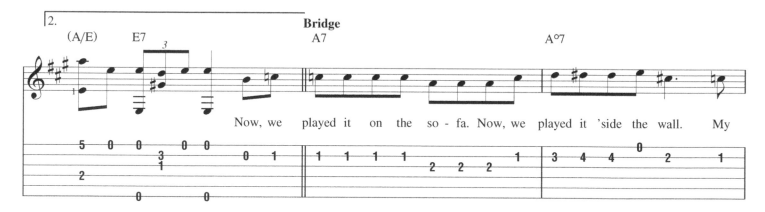

Now, we played it on the so - fa. Now, we played it 'side the wall. My

need - les have got rust - y, ba - by, they will not play at all. We played it on the

so-fa,   and we played it 'side the wall.

But my need-les have got rust-y,   and it will not play at all.

D.S. al Coda
(take repeat)

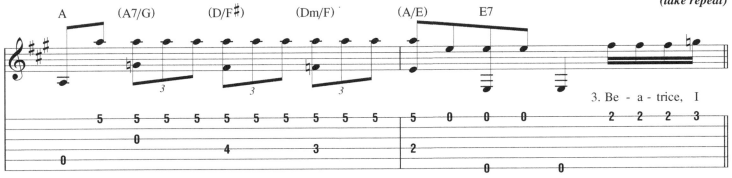

3. Be - a - trice, I

Coda

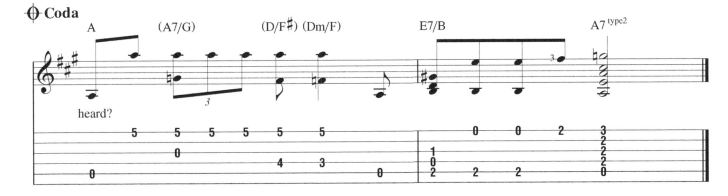

heard?

Additional Lyrics

2. Beatrice, I love my phonograph,
    But you have broke my windin' chain.
    Beatrice, I love my phonogra' ooo.
    Honey, I broke my windin' chain.
    And you've takin' my lovin'
    And gave it to your other man.

3. Beatrice, I go crazy.
    Baby, I will lose my mind.
    And I go cra'eee,
    Honey, I will lose my mind.
    Why-n't you bring your clothes back home
    And try me one more time?

4. She got a phonograph,
    And it won't say a lonesome word.
    She got a phonograph, ooo
    Won't say a lonesome word.
    What evil have I done, or
    What evil have the poor girl heard?

Ramblin' on my Mind

Words and Music by Robert Johnson

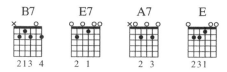

Strum Pattern: 1
Pick Pattern: 3

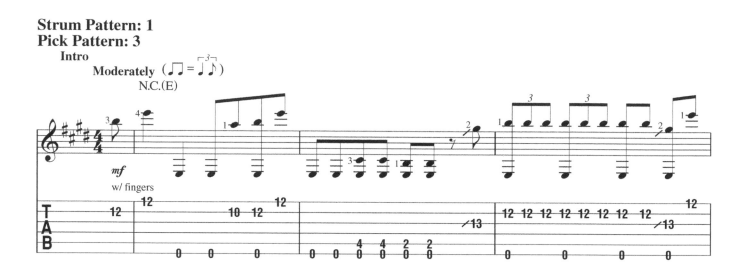

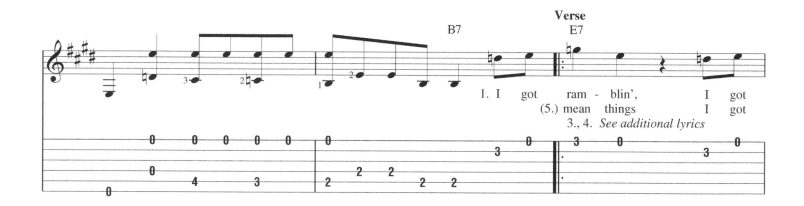

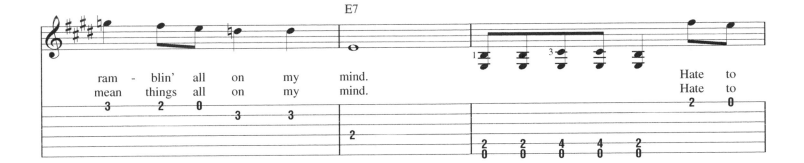

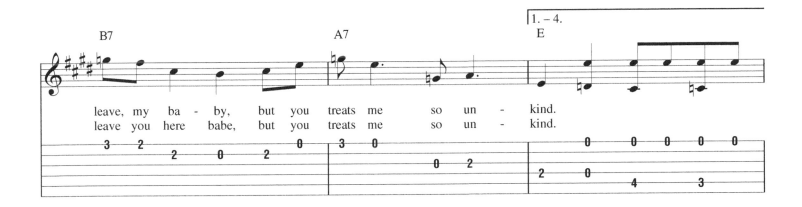

Additional Lyrics

3. Runnin' down to the station,
   Catch the first mail train I see.
Spoken: *I think I hear it comin' now.*
   Runnin' down to the station,
   Catch that old first mail train I see.
   I got the blues 'bout Miss So and So,
   And the child got the blues about me.

4. And I'm leavin' this mornin,'
   With my arm' fold' up and cry'n'.
   And I'm leavin' this mornin',
   With my arm' fold' upped and cry'n'.
   I hate to leave my baby,
   But she treats me so unkind.

Stones in My Passway

Words and Music by Robert Johnson

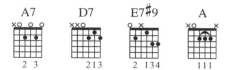

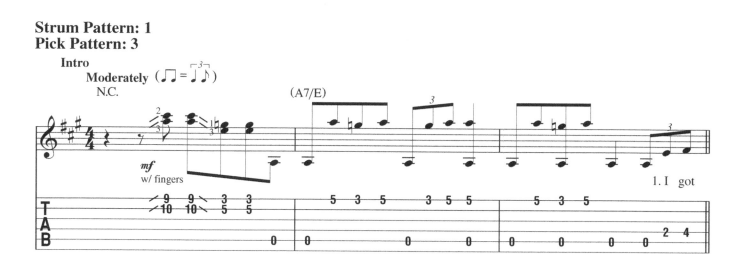

Strum Pattern: 1
Pick Pattern: 3

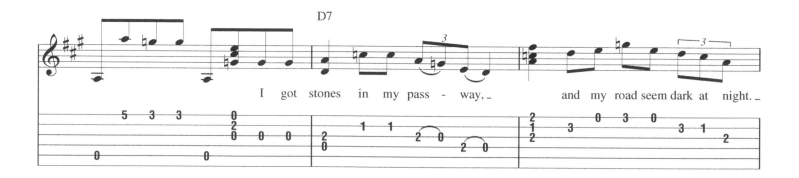

I have pains in my heart. _____

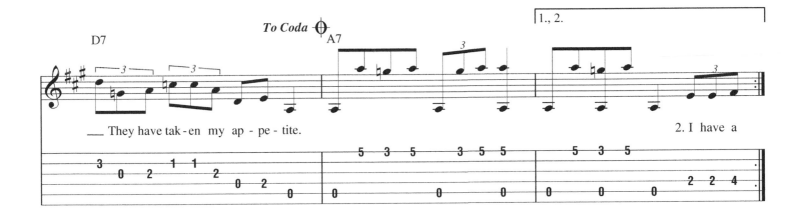

_ They have tak-en my ap - pe - tite.

2. I have a

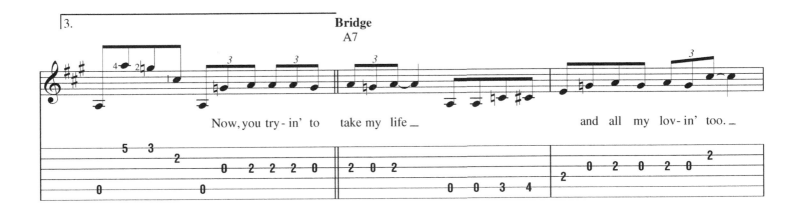

Now, you try-in' to take my life _ and all my lov-in' too. _

You laid a pass-way for me. Now what are you try - ing to do? I'm cry-in'

please, ___ plea - ease let us be friends. ___

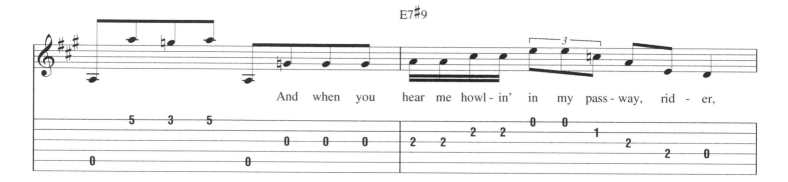

And when you hear me howl - in' in my pass - way, rid - er,

D.S. al Coda

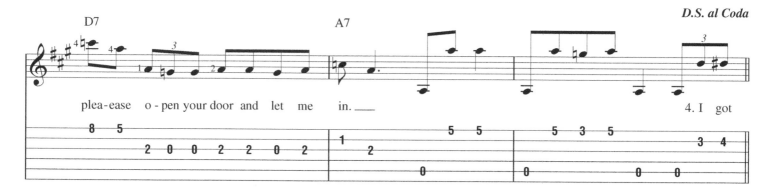

plea-ease o - pen your door and let me in. ___

4. I got

⊕ Coda

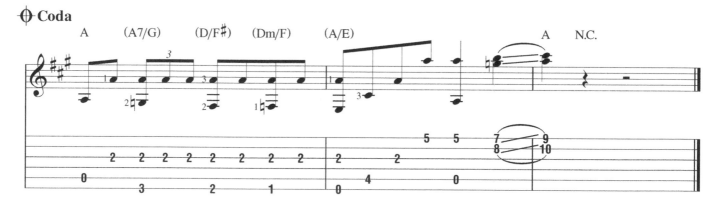

Additional Lyrics

2. I have a bird to whistle,
And I have a bird to sing.
Have a bird to whistle,
And I have a bird to sing.
I got a woman that I'm lovin',
Boy, but she don't mean a thing.

3. My enemies have betrayed me,
Have overtaken poor Bob at last.
My enemies have betrayed me,
Have overtaken poor Bob at last.
An' 'ere's one thing certainly,
They have stones in all my pass.

4. I got three legs to truck home.
Boys, please don't block my road.
I got three legs to truck home.
Boys, please don't block my road.
I've been feelin' ashamed 'bout my rider.
Babe, I'm booked and I got to go.

Sweet Home Chicago

Words and Music by Robert Johnson

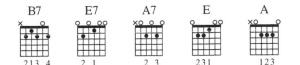

Strum Pattern: 1
Pick Pattern: 3

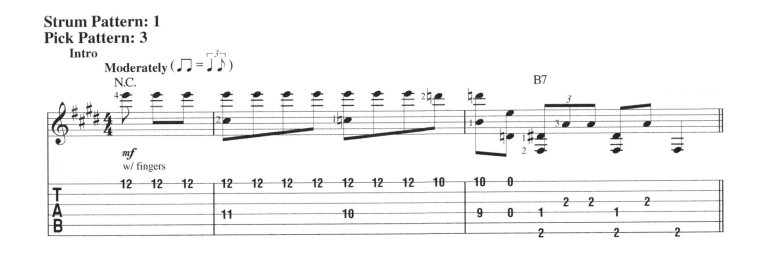

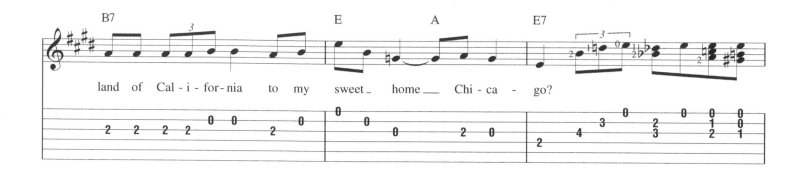

land of Cal-i-for-nia to my sweet home Chi-ca-go?

3. Now one and one is two.
two and two is four.
5., 6. *See additional lyrics*

Two and two is four. I'm heav-y load-ed ba-by. I'm
Four and two is six. You gon' keep on monk-ey'n' 'round here, friend-boy, gon'

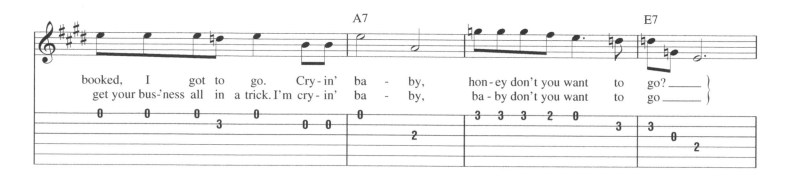

booked, I got to go. Cry-in' ba-by, hon-ey don't you want to go?
get your bus-'ness all in a trick. I'm cry-in' ba-by, ba-by don't you want to go

back to the land of Cal - i - for - nia, to my sweet home Chi - ca -

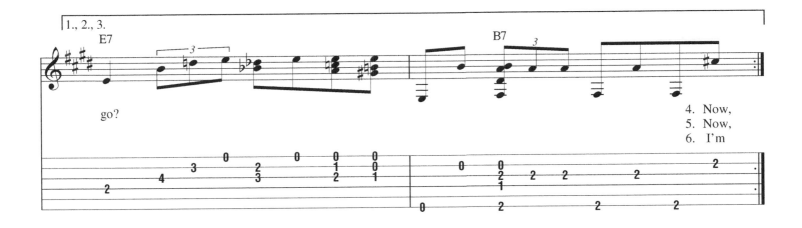

1., 2., 3.

go?

4. Now,
5. Now,
6. I'm

4.

go?

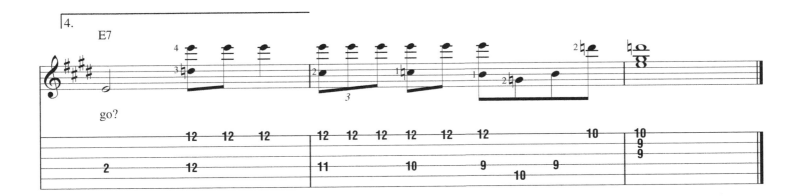

Additional Lyrics

5. Now, six and two is eight.
   Eight and two is ten.
   Friend-boy, she trick you one time, she sure gon' do it again.
   But I'm cryin' hey, hey, baby don't you want to go
   To the land of California,
   To my sweet home, Chicago?

6. I'm goin' to California.
   From there to Des Moines, I 'way.
   Somebody will tell me that you need my help someday.
   Cryin' hey, hey, baby don't you want to go,
   Back to the land of California,
   To my sweet home, Chicago?

They're Red Hot

Words and Music by Robert Johnson

Strum Pattern: 1
Pick Pattern: 3

Intro
Moderately fast

Verse

1., 9. Hot ta-mal-es and they're red hot. Yes, she got 'em for sale. Hot ta-mal-es and they're
2. – 8. *See additional lyrics*

red hot. Yes, she got 'em for sale. I got a girl, said she long and tall, she

sleeps in the kitch-en with her feets in the hall. Hot ta-mal-es and they're

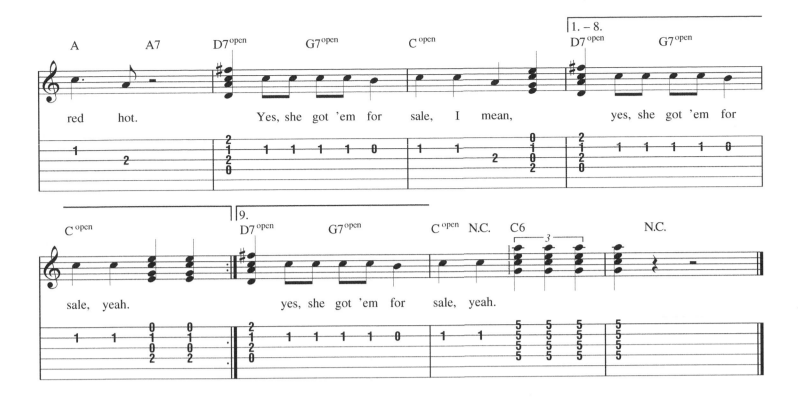

*Additional Lyrics

2. Hot tamales and they red hot.
   Yes, she got 'em for sale.
   Hot tamales and they red hot.
   Yes, she got 'em for sale.
   She got two for a nickel, got four for a dime.
   Would sell you more, but they ain't none of mine.
   Hot tamales and they red hot.
   Yes, she got 'em for sale.
   I mean, yes she got 'em for sale, yes, yeah.

3. Hot tamales and they red hot.
   Yes, she got 'em for sale.
   Hot tamales and they red hot.
   Yes, she got 'em for sale.
   I got a letter from a girl in the room.
   How, she got somethin' good she got to bring home soon, now.
   It's hot tamales and they red hot.
   Yes, she got 'em for sale.
   I mean, yes she got 'em for sale, yeah.

4. Hot tamales and they red hot.
   Yes, she got 'em for sale.
   Hot tamales and they red hot.
   Yes, she got 'em for sale. *They're too hot, boy!*
   The billy goat back' in a bumble bee nest.
   Ever since that, he can't take his rest, yeah.
   Hot tamales and they red hot.
   Yeah, you got 'em for sale.
   I mean, yes she got 'em for sale.

5. Hot tamales and they red hot.
   Yes, she got 'em for sale.
   Man, don't mess around 'em hot tamales, now
   'Cause they too black bad.
   If you mess around 'em hot tomales,
   I'm 'onna upset your backbone, put your kidneys to sleep.
   I'll due to break 'way your livin'
   And dare your heart to beat 'bout my
   Hot tamales 'cause they red hot.
   Yes, they got 'em for sale.
   I mean, yes she got 'em for sale, yeah.

6. Hot tamales and they red hot.
   Yes, she got 'em for sale.
   Hot tamales and they red hot.
   Yes, she got 'em for sale.
   You know grandma laughs, and now grandpa too.
   Well, I wonder what in the world we chillun gon' do, now.
   Hot tamales and they red hot.
   Yes, she got 'em for sale.
   I mean, yes she got 'em for sale.

7. Hot tamales and they red hot.
   Yes, she got 'em for sale.
   Hot tamales and they red hot.
   Yes, she got 'em for sale.
   Me and my babe bought a V-8 Ford.
   Well, we wind that thing all on the runnin' board, yes.
   Hot tamales and they red hot.
   Yes, she got 'em for sale.
   I mean, yes she got 'em for sale, yeah.

8. Hot tamales and they red hot.
   Yes, she got 'em for sale. *They're too hot, boy!*
   Hot tamales and they red hot.
   Yes, now, she got 'em for sale.
   You know the monkey, now the baboon playin' in the grass.
   Well, the monkey stuck his finger in that "Good Gulf Gas," now.
   Hot tamales and they red hot.
   Yes, she got 'em for sale.
   I mean, yes she got 'em for sale, yeah.

*Italicized lyrics are spoken.

Traveling Riverside Blues

Words and Music by Robert Johnson

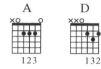

Strum Pattern: 1
Pick Pattern: 3

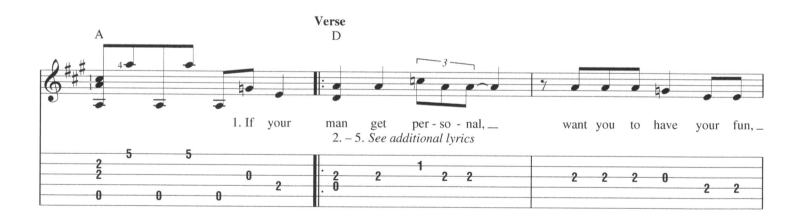

want you to have your fun, ____ just come on

back to Fri-ar's Point, ma-ma, and bar-rel-house all ____ night ____

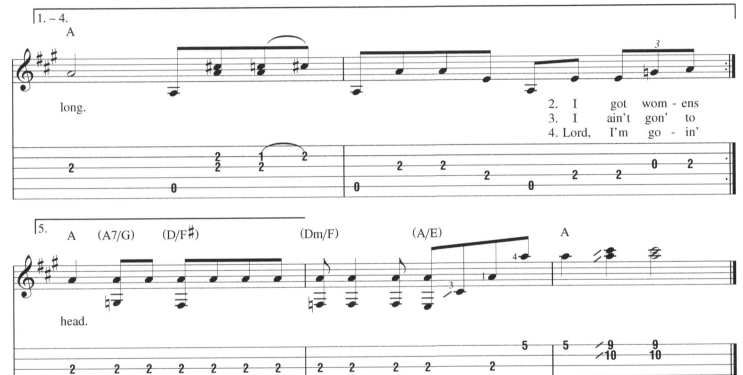

1. – 4.

long.

2. I got wom-ens
3. I ain't gon' to
4. Lord, I'm go-in'

5.

head.

Additional Lyrics

2. I got womens in Vicksburg,
   Clean on into Tennessee.
   I got womens in Vicksburg,
   Clean on into Tennessee,
   But my Friar's Point rider, now,
   Hops all over me.

3. I ain't gon' to state no color,
   But her front teeth crowned with gold.
   I ain't gon' to state no color,
   But her front teeth is crowned with gold.
   She got a mortgage on my body, now,
   And a lien on my soul.

4. Lord, I'm goin' to Rosedale,
   Gonna take my rider by my side.
   Lord, I'm goin' to Rosedale,
   Gon' take my rider by my side.
   We can still barrelhouse, baby,
   'Cause it's on the riverside.

5. Now, you can squeeze my lemon
   'Til the juice run down my...
   Spoken: 'Til the juice run down my leg, baby.
   You know what I'm talkin' 'bout.
   You can squeeze my lemon
   'Til the juice run down my leg.
   Spoken: That's what I'm talkin' 'bout, now.
   But I'm goin' back to Friar's Point,
   If I be rockin' to my head.

Walkin' Blues

Words and Music by Robert Johnson

Strum Pattern: 1
Pick Pattern: 3

Intro
Moderately

N.C.(A)

mf
w/ fingers

(A7/G)   (D/F#)   (Dm/F)

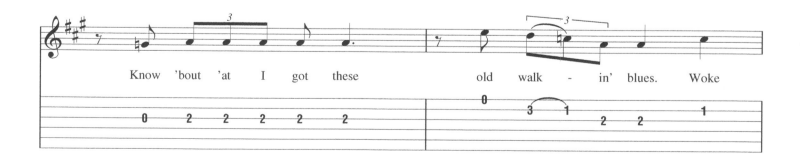

(A/E)   **Verse**
A

1. I woke up this morn - in,' ___ feel-in' 'round for my shoes.
2. – 5. *See additional lyrics*

Know 'bout 'at I got these old walk - in' blues. Woke

up this morn - in', _____ feel - in' 'round oh, for my shoes. _

___ But you know' ____ 'bout 'at I ____

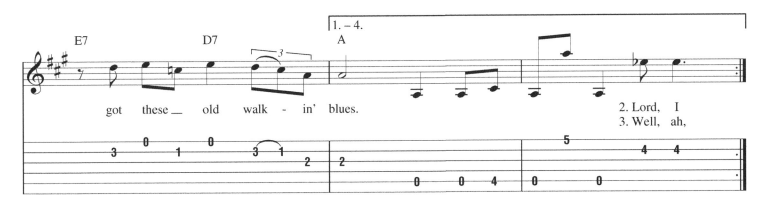

got these __ old walk - in' blues. 2. Lord, I
3. Well, ah,

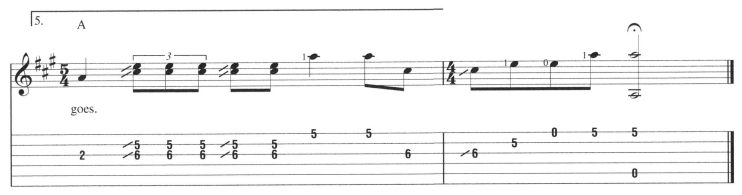

goes.

Additional Lyrics

2. Lord, I feel like blowin' my old lonesome horn.
   Got up this mornin', my little Bernice was gone.
   Lord, I feel like blow-ooon' my lonesome horn.
   Well, I got up this mornin', all I had was gone.

3. Well, leave this norn' if I have to woh, ride the blind, ah.
   I've feel mistreated and I don't mind dy'n'.
   Leave this morn', ah, I have to ride a blind.
   Babe, I been mistreated, baby, and I don't mind dyin'.

4. Well, some people tell me that the worried blues ain't bad.
   Worst old feelin' I most ever had.
   Some people tell me that these old worried old blues ain't bad.
   It's the worst old feelin' I most ever had.

5. She got a Elgin movement from her head down to her toes.
   Break in on a dollar most anywhere she goes.
   Ooo, to her head down to her toes.
   Spoken: Oh, honey.
   Lord, she break in on a dollar most anywhere she goes.

When You Got a Good Friend

Words and Music by Robert Johnson

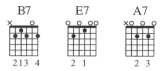

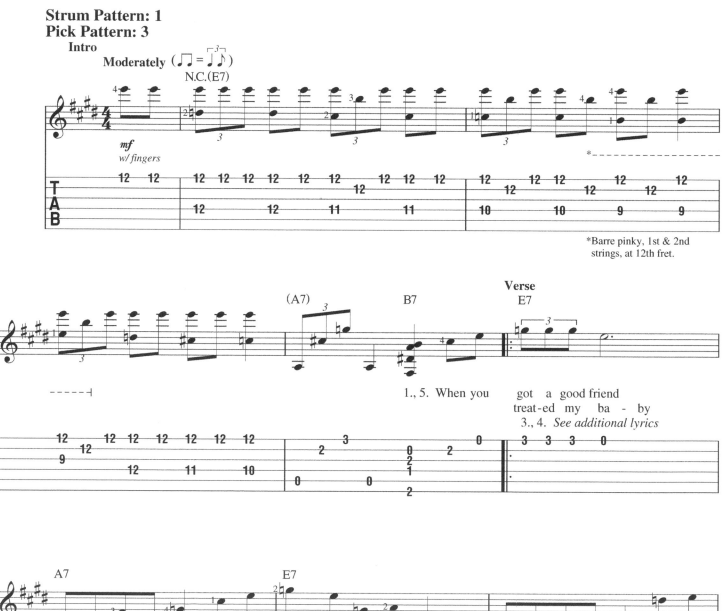

*Barre pinky, 1st & 2nd
strings, at 12th fret.

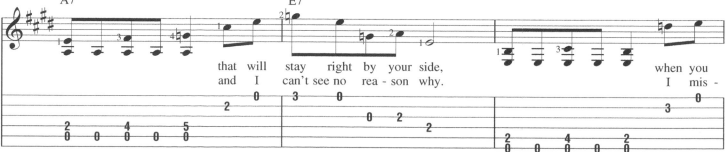

got a good friend that will stay right by your side,
treat-ed my ba - by and I can't see no rea - son why.

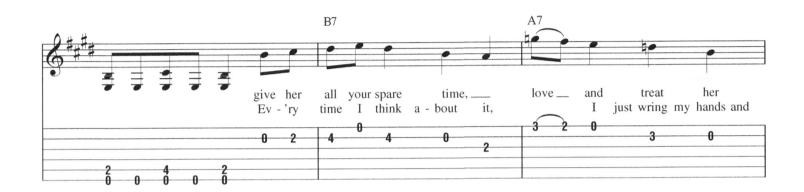

give her all your spare time, ___ love ___ and treat her
Ev - 'ry time I think a - bout it, I just wring my hands and

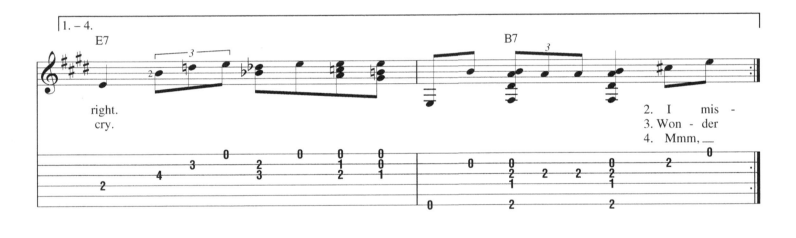

right.
cry.

2. I mis -
3. Won - der
4. Mmm, ___

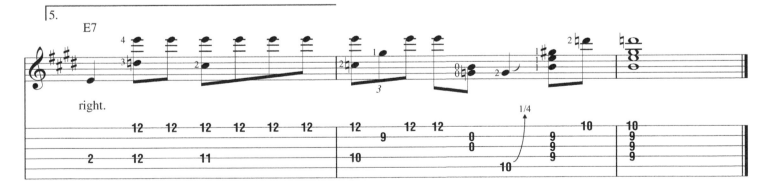

right.

Additional Lyrics

3. Wonder, could I bear apologize,
   Or would she sympathize with me?
   Mmm,
   Would she sympathize with me?
   She's a brown-skin woman,
   Just as sweet as a girl friend can be.

4. Mmm,
   Babe, I may be right a wrong.
   Baby, it's your opinion,
   Oh, I may be right as wrong.
   Watch your close friend, baby,
   Then your enemies can't do you no harm.

Terraplane Blues

Words and Music by Robert Johnson

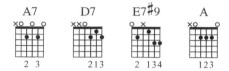

A7   D7   E7#9   A

Strum Pattern: 1
Pick Pattern: 3

Intro
Moderately

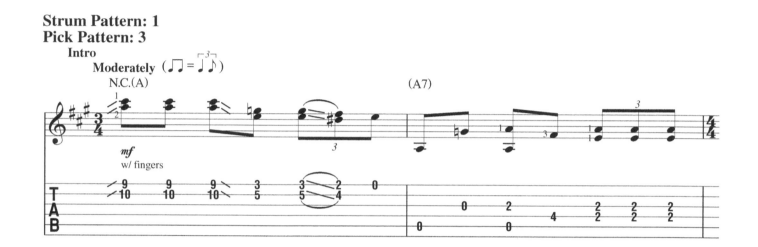

N.C.(A)   (A7)

mf
w/ fingers

Verse
A7

1. And I feel so lone - some, ___ you hear me when I moan. ___
2. – 6. *See additional lyrics*

D7

When I feel so lone - some,

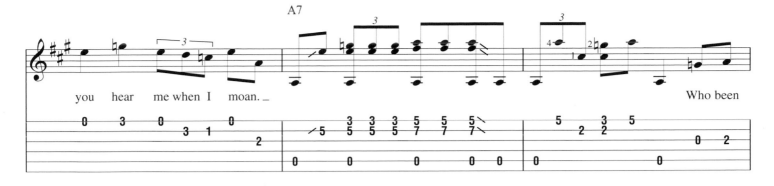

you hear me when I moan. _ Who been

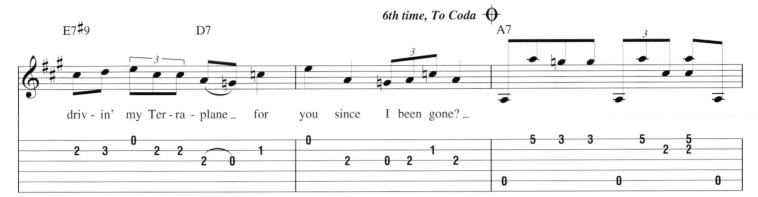

6th time, To Coda

driv - in' my Ter - ra - plane _ for you since I been gone? _

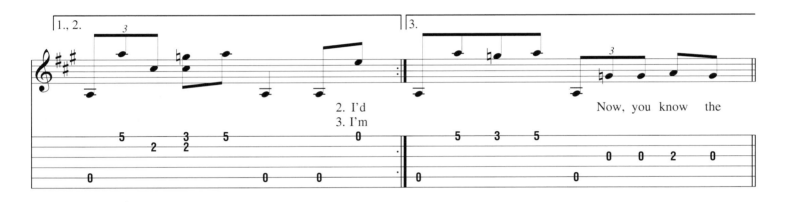

2. I'd
3. I'm

Now, you know the

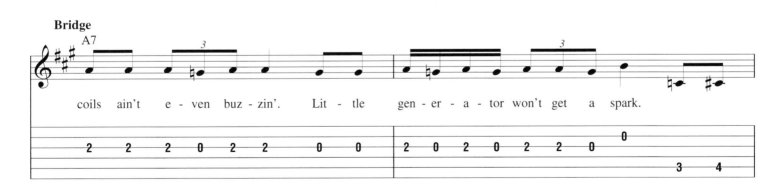

Bridge

coils ain't e - ven buz - zin'. Lit - tle gen - er - a - tor won't get a spark.

Mot - or's in a bad con - di - tion. You got - ta have these bat - t'ries charged. But I'm cry'n'

please, ____ plea - hease don't do me wrong. ___

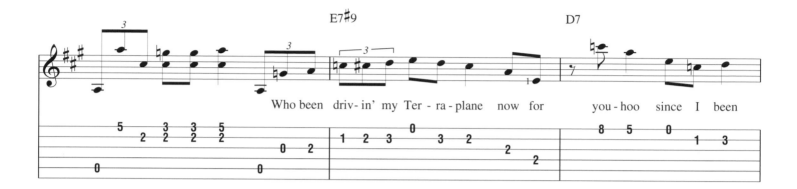

Who been driv-in' my Ter-ra-plane now for you-hoo since I been

D.S. al Coda
(take repeats)

⊕ **Coda**

gone? _ 4. Mis - ter

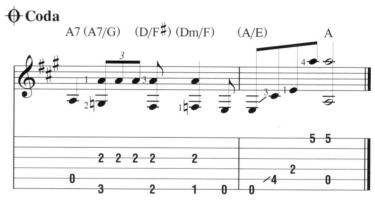

Additional Lyrics

2. I'd said I flash your lights, mama.
   Your horn won't even blow.
   Spoken: Somebody's been runnin' my batteries down on this machine.
   I even flash my lights, mama.
   This horn won't even blow.
   Got a short in this connection.
   Hoo-well, babe, it's way down below.

3. I'm 'on' h'ist your hood, mama.
   I'm bound to check your oil.
   I'm gon' h'ist your hood, mama.
   I'm bound to check your oil.
   I got a woman that I'm lovin'
   Way down in Arkansas.

4. Mister Highwayman,
   Plea-hease don't block the road.
   Puh hee hee,
   Plea-hease don't block the road.
   'Cause she re'ist'rin' a cold one hundred
   And I'm booked and I gotta go.

5. Mmm, mmm.
   Mmm, mmm.
   You,
   You hear me weep and moan.
   Who been drivin' my Terraplane now for
   You hoo since I been gone?

6. I'm 'on' get deep down in this connection,
   Keep on tanglin' with your wires.
   I'm 'on' get deep down in this connection,
   Hoo well, keep on tanglin' with these wires.
   And when I mash down on your little starter,
   Then your spark plug will give me fire.